DANGEROUS DISEASES

Measles

by Rebecca Pettiford

BLASTOFF! READERS 3

BLASTOFF! READERS, AN IMPRINT OF BELLWETHER MEDIA BY FLUTTERBEE

Blastoff! Readers are carefully developed by literacy experts to build reading stamina and move students toward fluency by combining standards-based content with developmentally appropriate text.

LEVELS

Level 1 provides the most support through repetition of high-frequency words, light text, predictable sentence patterns, and strong visual support.

Level 2 offers early readers a bit more challenge through varied sentences, increased text load, and text-supportive special features.

Level 3 advances early-fluent readers toward fluency through increased text load, less reliance on photos, advancing concepts, longer sentences, and more complex special features.

★ **Blastoff! Universe**

Reading Level

Blastoff! Beginners — Grade K

Blastoff! Readers — Grades 1–3

Blastoff! Discovery — Grade 4

This edition first published in 2027 by Bellwether Media, Inc.

For information regarding permission, write to Bellwether Media, Inc., Attention: Permissions Department, 3500 American Blvd W, Suite 150, Bloomington, MN 55431.

Library of Congress Cataloging-in-Publication Data is available at www.loc.gov or upon request from the publisher.

ISBN: 9798898800673 (hardcover)
ISBN: 9798898801915 (ebook)

Editor: Suzane Nguyen Designer: Brittany McIntosh

Printed in the United States of America, North Mankato, MN.

Table of Contents

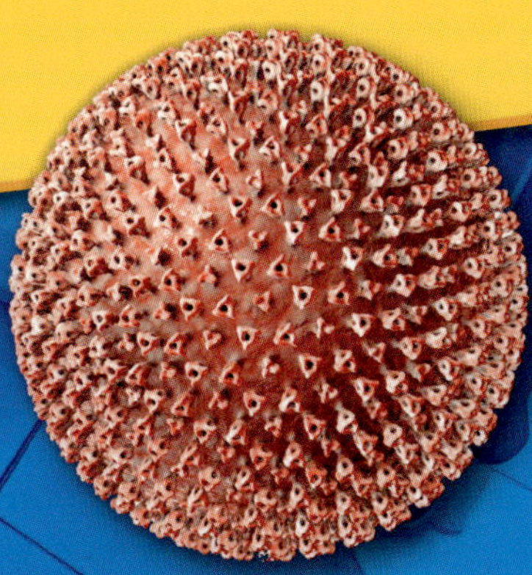

What Is Measles?

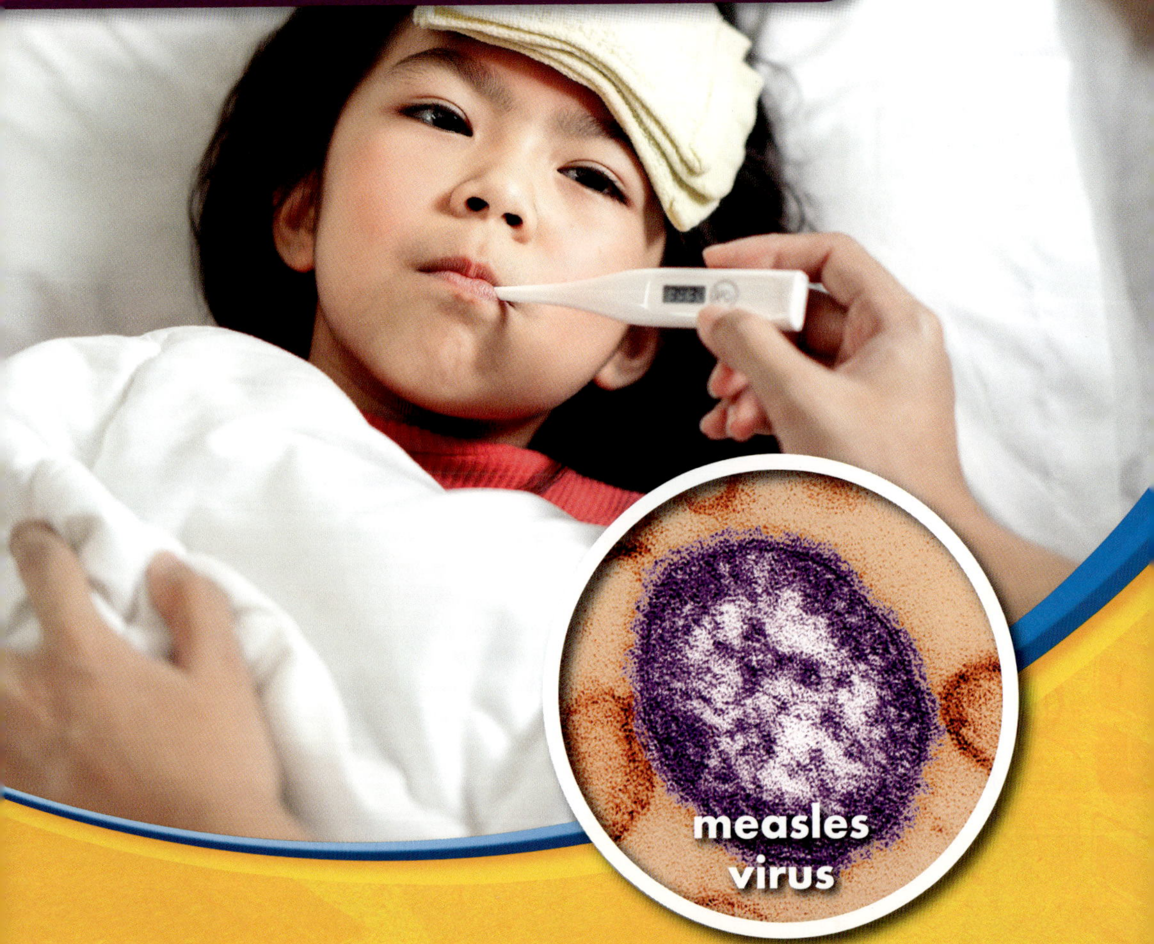

Measles is caused by a **virus**. Early signs include a **fever** and cough. Other signs are a runny nose and red eyes.

Later a **rash** appears on the **forehead**. It spreads to the rest of the body.

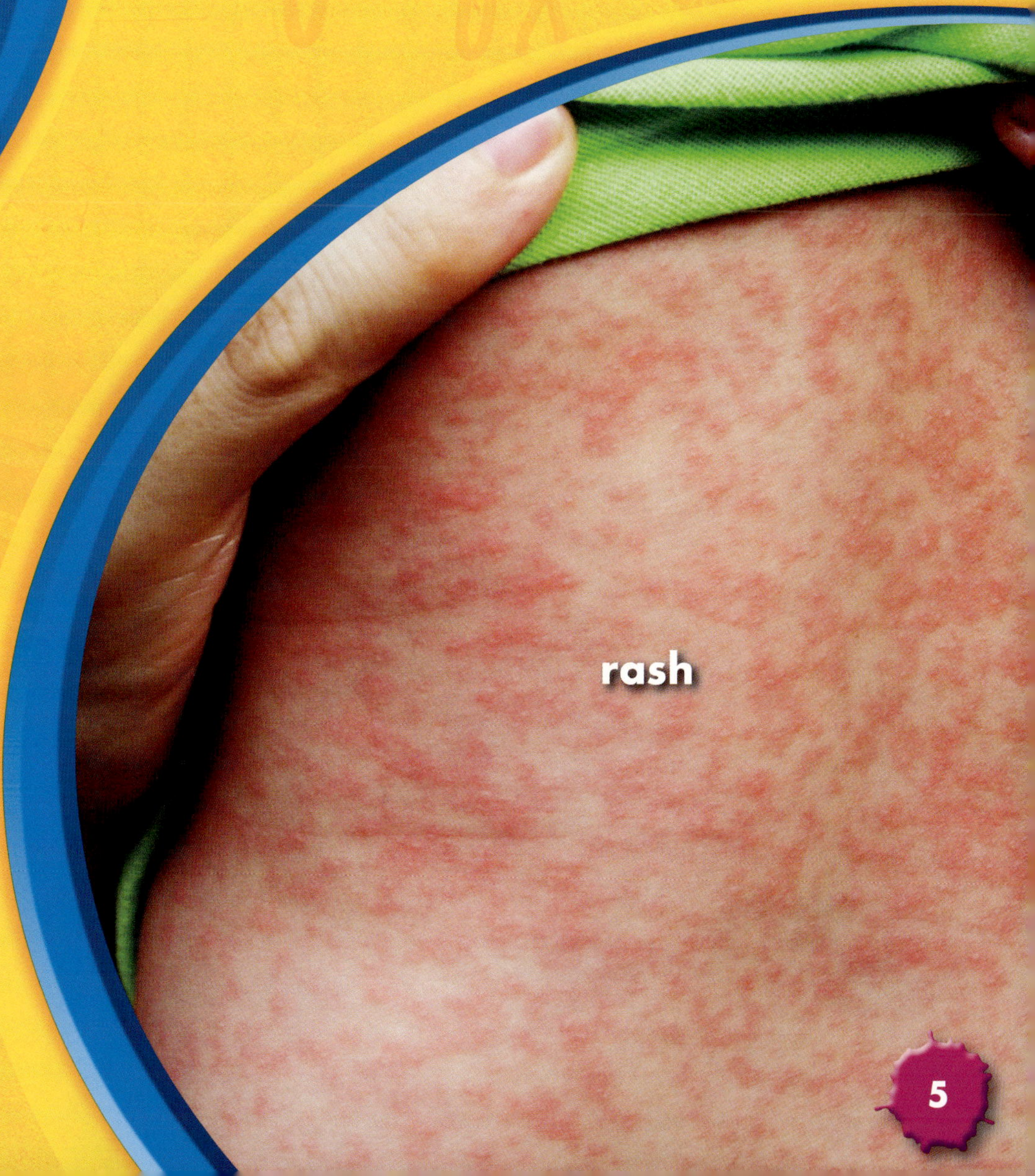

Measles used to affect nearly four million people in the United States each year. Today, most people are **vaccinated**.

getting vaccinated

New Outbreaks

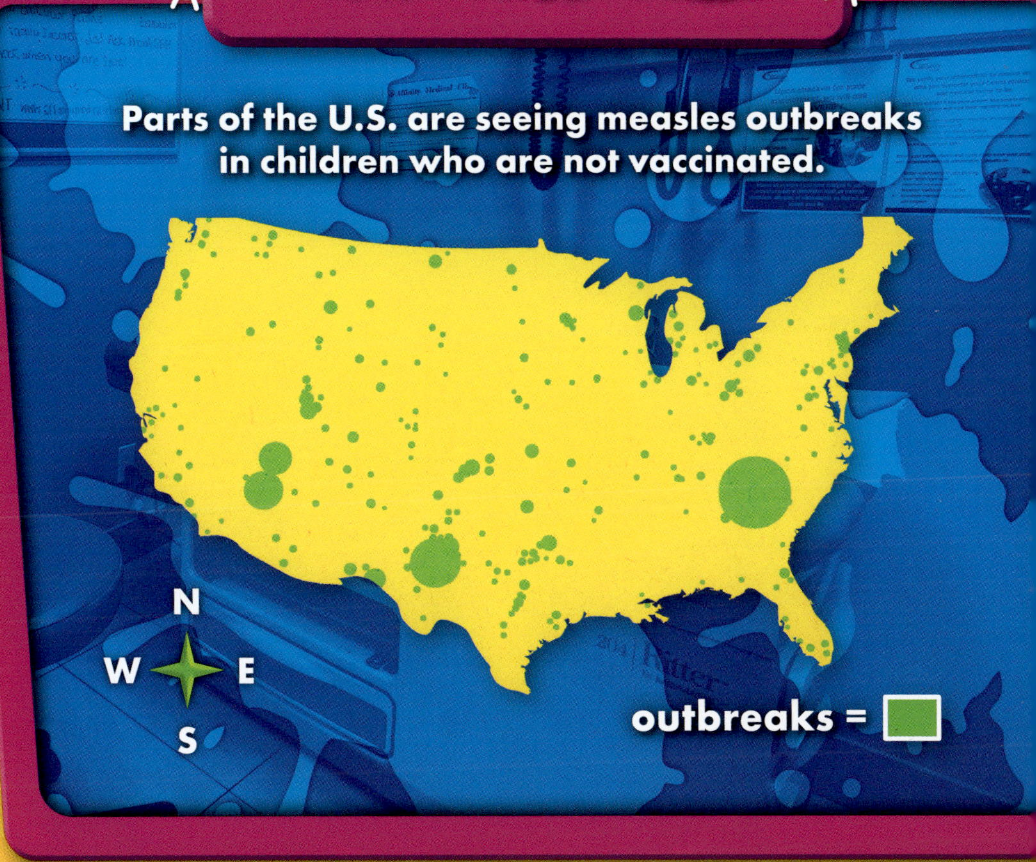

In parts of the world, **outbreaks** can happen when people are not vaccinated.

History of Measles

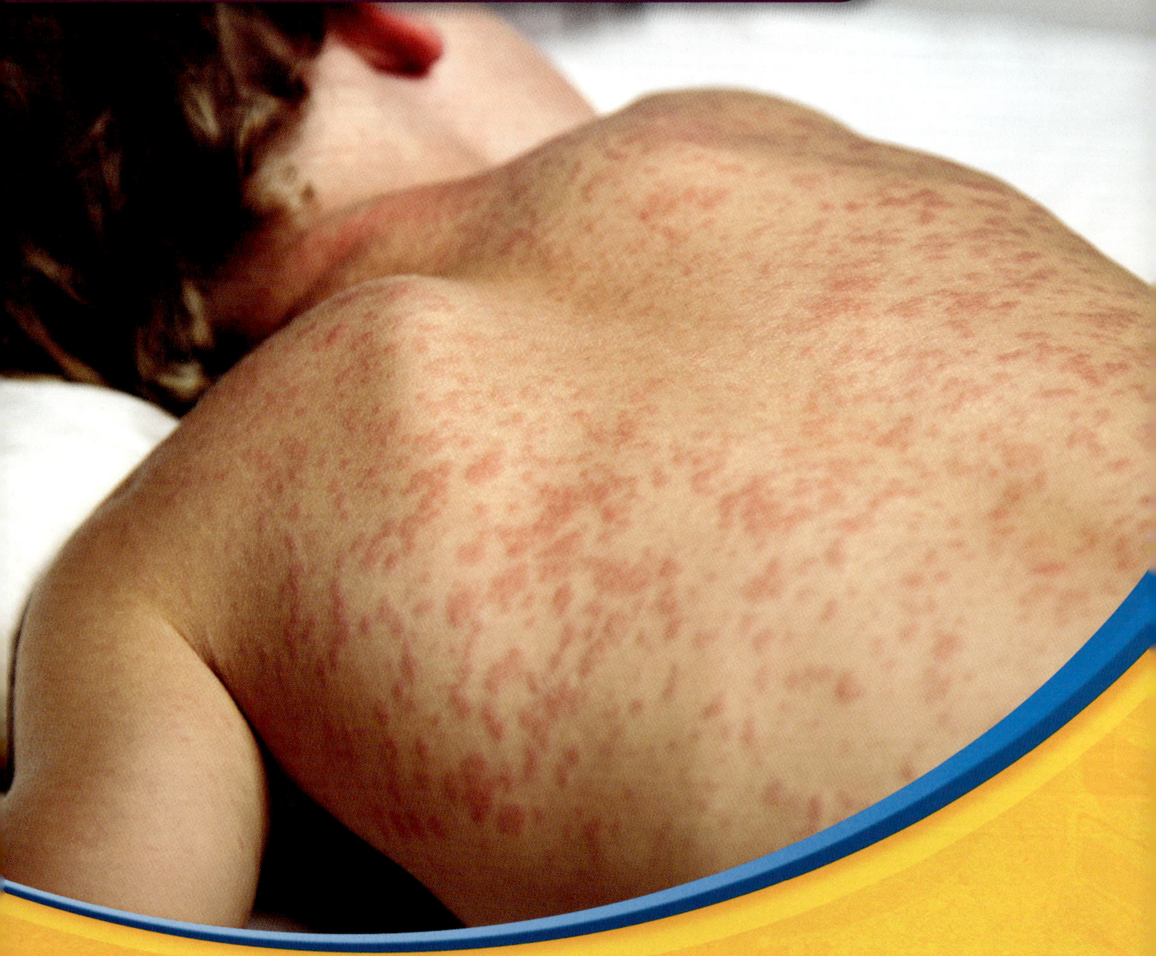

Measles has been around for over a thousand years.

In 1757, a Scottish doctor found what caused measles. He tried to make a vaccine for it.

Scottish doctor, Francis Home

In 1954, two doctors in the U.S. **isolated** the virus. One of them made the first measles vaccine in 1963.

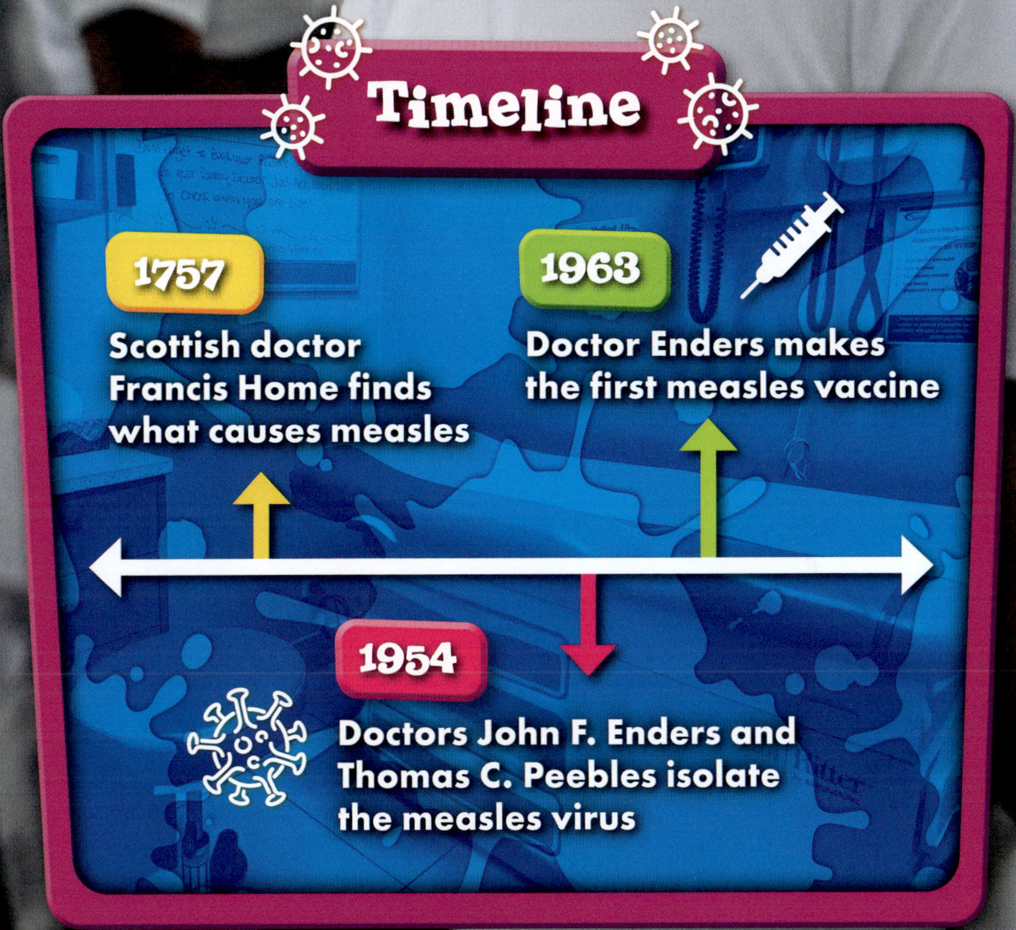

About 60 million people worldwide between 2000 and 2024 have been saved by the vaccine.

How Does Measles Spread?

Measles is very **contagious**. It can spread when a person who has it coughs or sneezes.

Droplets from the cough or sneeze move through the air.

Some people are not **immune**. They breathe in the droplets. They touch things that have droplets on them. They get sick.

The first signs of measles often show up within 14 days.

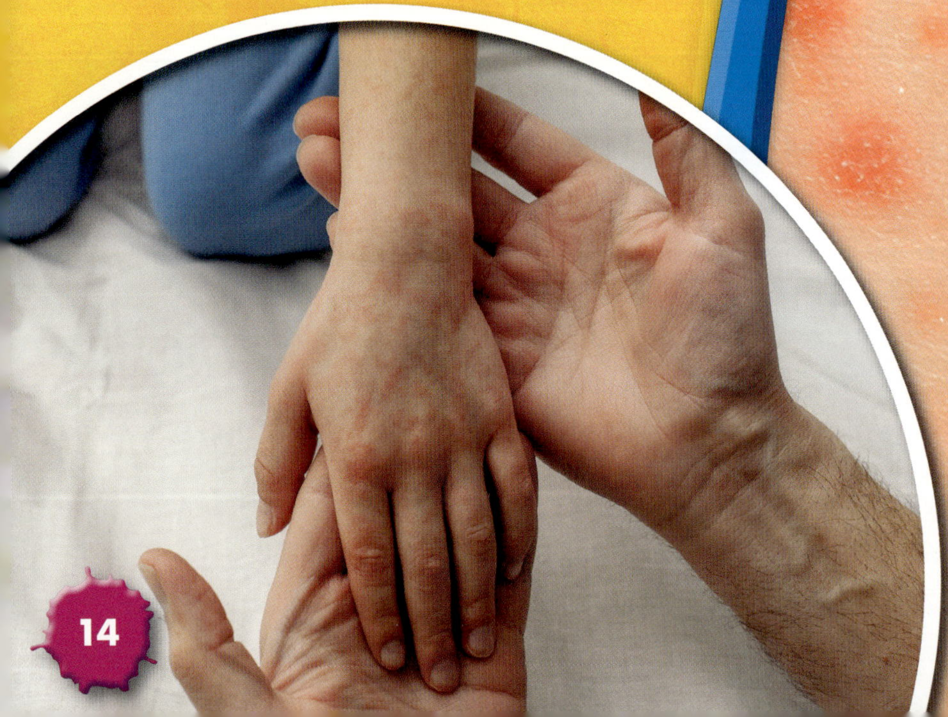

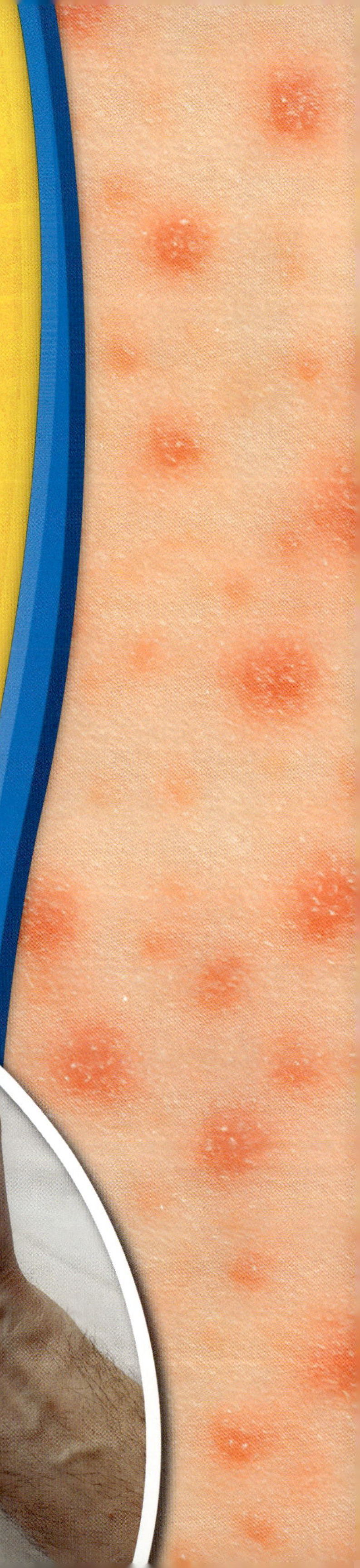

How Measles Spreads

By Air

1

Someone coughs or sneezes.

2
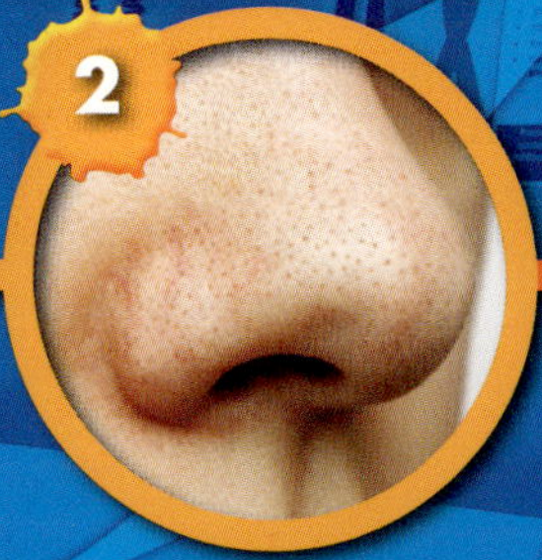

Droplets in the air enter a person's mouth or nose.

3
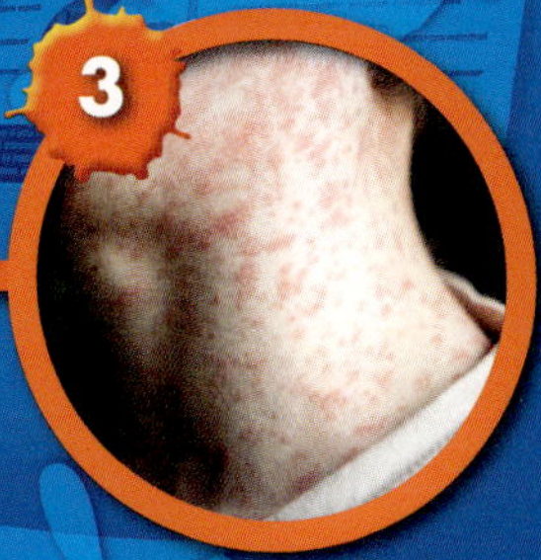

Person gets measles.

By Touch

1

Virus on object.

2

Person touches object.

3
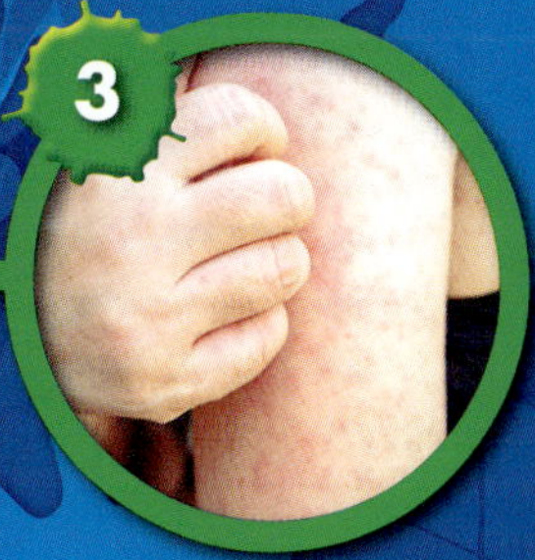

Person gets measles.

Prevention and Treatment

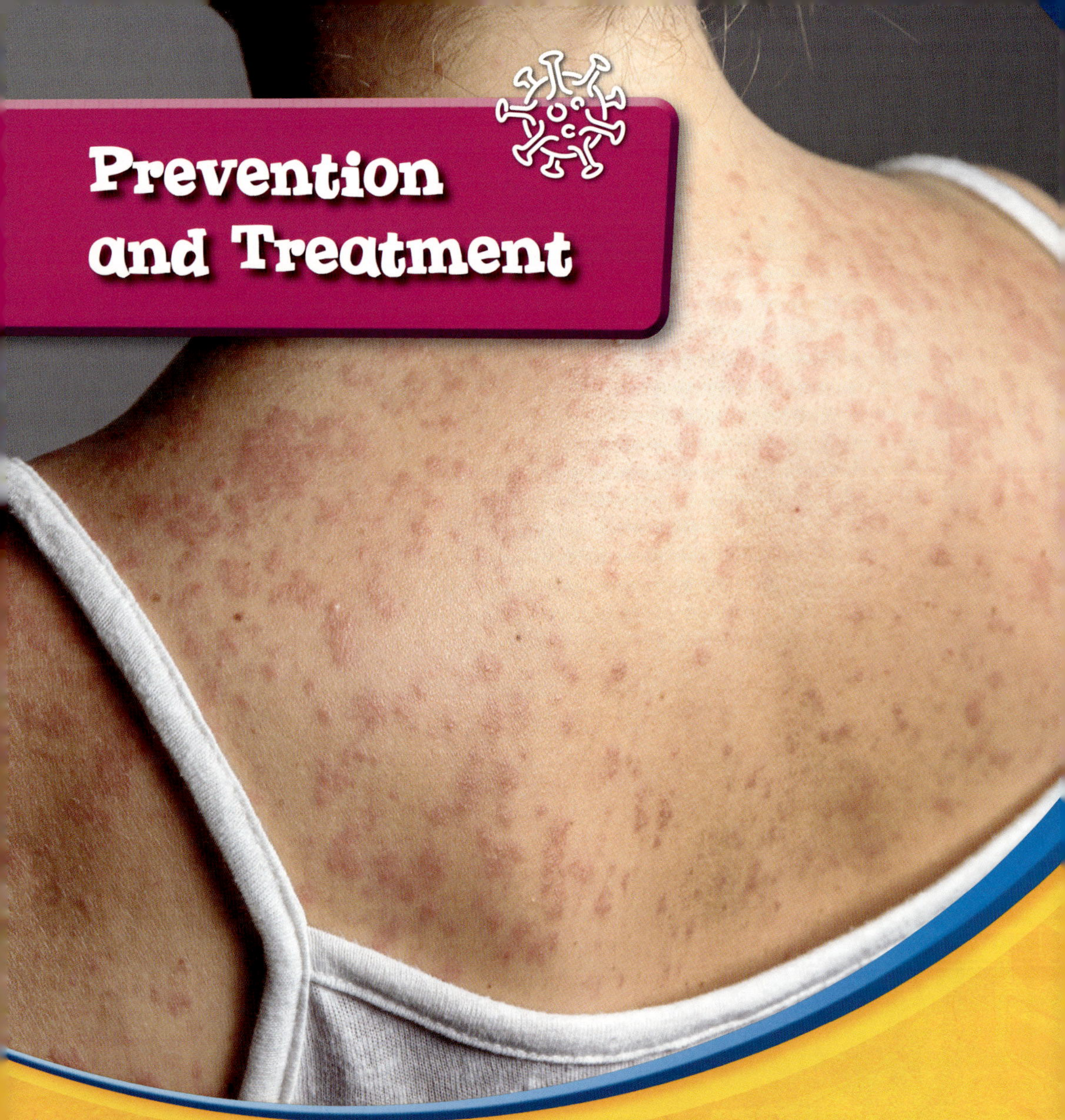

Measles is more common in children. But adults can get it too.

Sick people need lots of rest. They should drink plenty of liquids. It can take about two weeks to feel better.

Getting vaccinated is the best way to stay well. The vaccine is a weak form of the virus.

Healing Hero

Name

Doctor John F. Enders

Year Helped

1963

How He Helped

Doctor Enders made the first measles vaccine.

It causes the **immune system** to make **antibodies**.

There is no cure for measles.

But once people have had it, they are immune to it for the rest of their lives!

Glossary

antibodies–materials that the body makes to fight illnesses

contagious–able to spread

fever–a higher-than-normal body temperature

forehead–the part of the face above the eyes

immune–unable to get sick easily

immune system–the system that proects the body from illnesses

isolated–separated from its surroundings

outbreaks–sudden sudden increase in cases of a disease

rash–an area of itchy, red spots on the skin

vaccinated–having gotten a vaccine; a vaccine is a substance that is put into the body to help fight off an illness.

virus–a tiny living thing that causes illness in people, animals, and plants

To Learn More

AT THE LIBRARY

Pettiford, Rebecca. *Chickenpox*. Minneapolis, Minn.: Bellwether Media, 2027.

Redford, Ruth. *The Measles Files*. Rochester, Minn.: Mayo Clinic Press Kids, 2026.

Troupe, Thomas Kingsley. *What Would Happen If You Never Got Vaccines?* Mankato, Minn.: Amicus Learning, 2024.

ON THE WEB

FACTSURFER

Factsurfer.com gives you a safe, fun way to find more information.

1. Go to www.factsurfer.com.
2. Enter "measles" into the search box and click .
3. Select your book cover to see a list of related content.

Index

The images in this book are reproduced through the courtesy of: Kateryna Kon, front cover (hero), p. 3; Natalya_Maisheva, front cover (splatter right); Maria Sbytova, front cover (splatter left); Habanero Pixel, front cover (background); Chanintorn.v, p. 4; Connect Images/ Alamy Stock Photo, p. 4 (inset); phichet chaiyabin, p. 5; Mohammed al-wafi, p. 6; Aleksandr Finch, p. 8; David Allan/ Wikipedia, p. 9; YURI CORTEZ/ Contributor/ Getty Images, pp. 10-11; cunaplus, p. 12; pabst_ell, p. 13; olvius, p. 14; DRMEK, pp. 14-15; Art_Photo, p. 15 (by air 1); Marina Demeshko, p. 15 (by air 2); Natalya_Maisheva, p. 15 (by air 3); chainarong06, p. 15 (by touch 1); BongkarnGraphic, p. 15 (by touch 2); SingjaiStocker, p. 15 (by touch 3); Efired, p. 16; Mariana, p. 17; Arlette Lopez, p. 18; ustas7777777, p. 18 (inset); Bettmann/ Contributor/ Getty Images, p. 19; _jure, p. 20; Forewer, p. 21.